OPEN THIS BOOK

(in the event of boredom)

OPEN THIS BOOK

(in the event of boredom)

Louis Catlett

SIRIUS

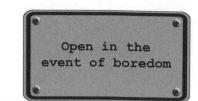

Open in the
event of boredom

SIRIUS

This edition published in 2022 by Sirius Publishing, a division of
Arcturus Publishing Limited,
26/27 Bickels Yard, 151–153 Bermondsey Street,
London SE1 3HA

ISBN: 978-1-3988-2099-9
AD010662NT

Printed in China

CONTENTS

OPEN THIS BOOK IN THE EVENT OF BOREDOM

So, you've opened this book...

Congratulations on taking the first step on your journey to boredom relief. Please take a seat and fill out this form, then continue to the next page. Then proceed to the page after that, and so on and so forth until you run out of pages, pencils, or patience.

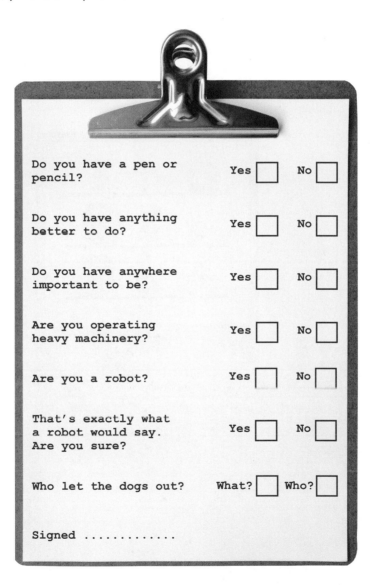

Do you have a pen or pencil? Yes ☐ No ☐

Do you have anything better to do? Yes ☐ No ☐

Do you have anywhere important to be? Yes ☐ No ☐

Are you operating heavy machinery? Yes ☐ No ☐

Are you a robot? Yes ☐ No ☐

That's exactly what a robot would say. Are you sure? Yes ☐ No ☐

Who let the dogs out? What? ☐ Who? ☐

Signed . . . .

NEVER-ENDING VENDING

If you had a fully stocked vending machine in your house, with a completely free, never-ending supply of nine things, what would they be?

The items don't have to be food or drink, but the machine can't stock money and none of the items that come out of it can be resold.

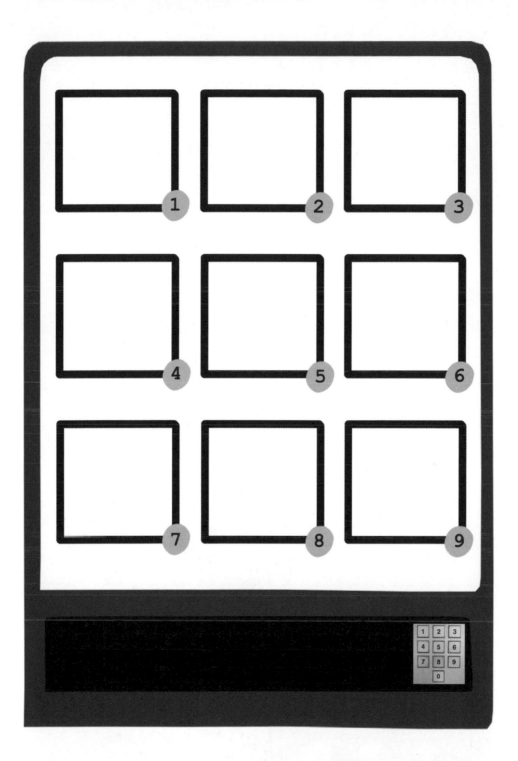

ALTERNATE ACRONYMS

It can be hard to keep up with the number of acronyms that have worked their way into everyday use. Come up with your own phrases to fit these acronyms and give them a whole new meaning.

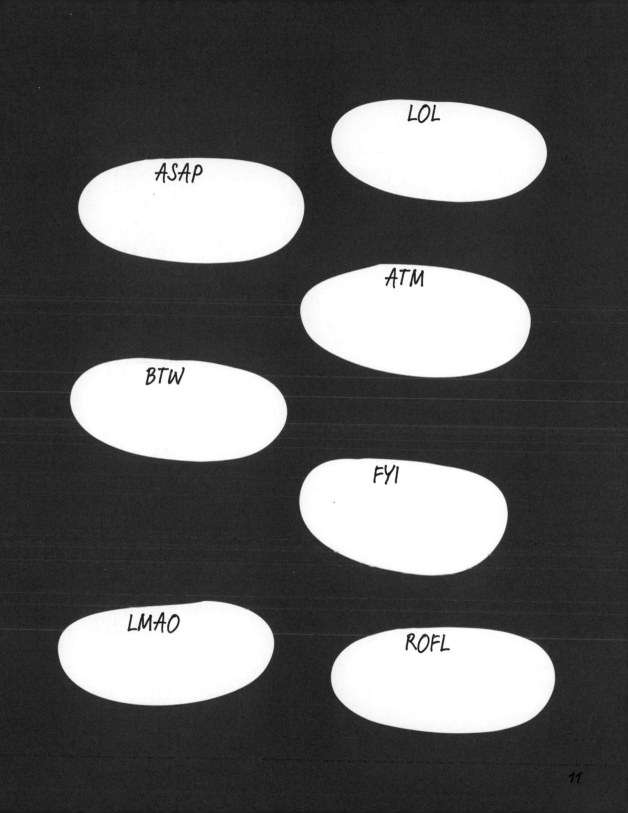

THE SEAL OF FORTUNE

Some vague nuggets of ill-informed wisdom brought to you by a semi-aquatic mammal in a sparkly hat.

Drop your pen onto this wheel from a height to decide your fortune.

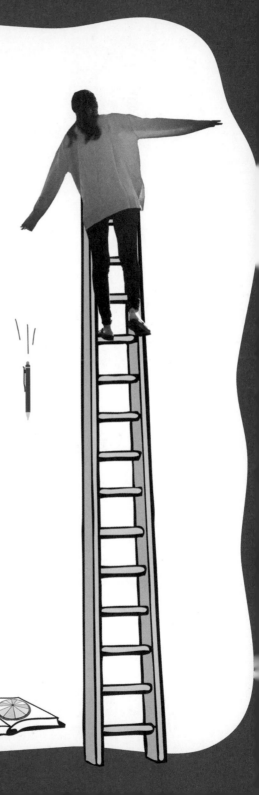

ALTERED MOVIE TITLES

Make subtle changes to movie titles to give them a new meaning and fill out the table with your funniest.

CHANGE ONE LETTER REMOVE ONE LETTER

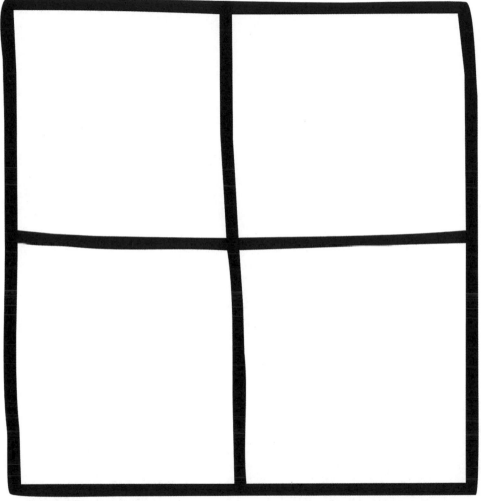

REMOVE ONE LETTER
+ CHANGE ONE LETTER

ADD ONE LETTER +
CHANGE ONE LETTER

FANTASY GROUP CHAT

Which famous folk would make for an interesting group chat dynamic? What would be their opening lines to one another? What would they name their group?

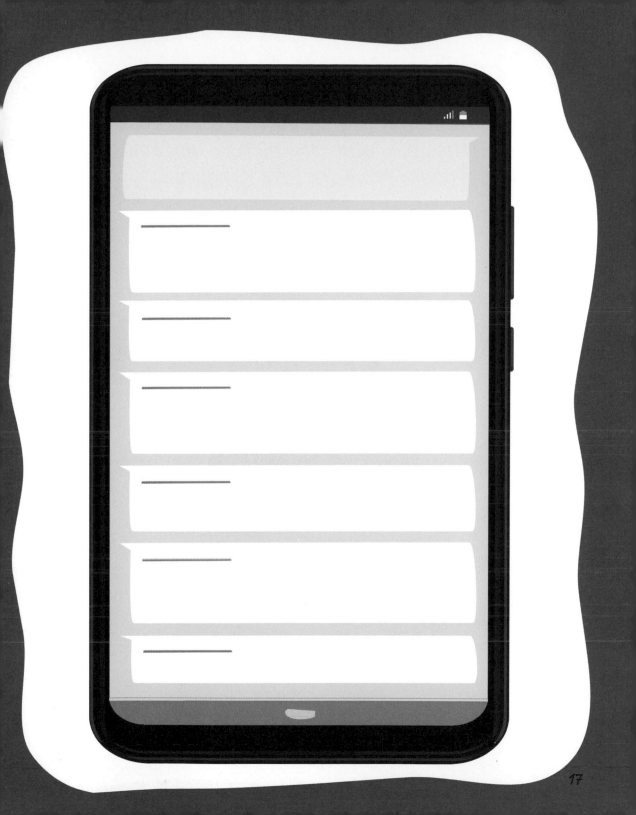

THE LOVE KANGURU

Add your first initial to your partner's and receive some questionable and completely unfounded relationship advice from the Love Kanguru.

A = 4 F = 1 K = 6 P = 6 U = 1
B = 1 G = 1 L = 3 Q = 1 V = 3
C = 5 H = 5 M = 3 R = 6 W = 5
D = 3 I = 6 N = 6 S = 2 X = 1
E = 6 J = 2 O = 2 T = 5 Y = 4
                              Z = 6

2 – Your love will resemble a firework display. Short-lived and a waste of money.

3 – This relationship will put the "fun" in dysfunctional.

4 – The only thing you have in common is your disdain for one another.

5 – They say opposites attract. But that's really about magnets and shouldn't be applied to love.

6 – This relationship will be a walk in the park. But the park is actually a maze. And it's on fire.

7 – As matches go, you're one of the ones that breaks on the side of the packet before lighting.

8 – You'll make an awesome couple! Sorry, autocorrect... *Awful.

9 – Your love resembles a rocky road. A literal one though. Not the nice one with marshmallows in. One with actual rocks.

10 – This fiery relationship will be love at first fight.

11 – They say two wrongs don't make a right. This is no exception.

12 – If you're seeking relationship validation from a fictional kangaroo in a book then I think you should just call it a day.

TO THE MOON AND PACK!

You're off on a trip to the moon tomorrow, but the budget airline you're flying with is only permitting you to take five items on board. Your accommodation is all-inclusive so any bare essentials are covered. You are there for six months though and there's not a lot to do on the moon. What are you putting in your case?

WHAT'S ON YOUR MIND?

Annotate this brain with the top ten things that occupy yours on a daily basis.

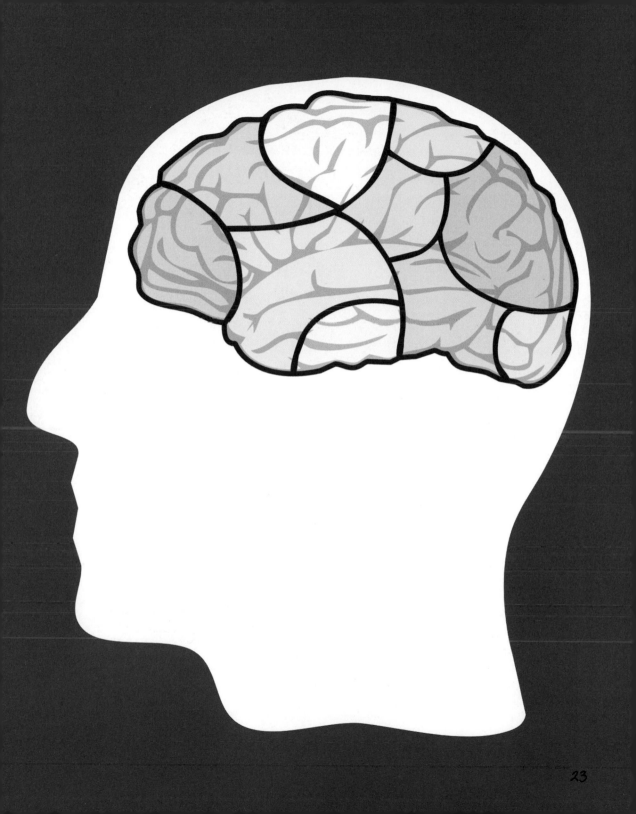

23

THE ULTIMATE SUPER GROUP

who would play in your dream band?

VOCALS:

KEYS:

GUITAR:

DANCER:

DRUMS:

BASS:

25

WHICH CONDIMENT ARE YOU?

Ketchups are the trustworthy and dependable companion that's there when you need them. They get on well with everyone and always have your back. Ketchups are a welcome guest at social events.

Mustards are an acquired taste. They do their own thing and quietly get on with life keeping themselves to themselves. They keep a few friends close but don't tend to socialize often.

Mayos are loyal and laid-back. They try very hard to blend in and not offend anyone, but are somehow still disliked by some. Nothing seems to phase an easygoing mayo though, so they keep a cool head and shrug off the hate.

BBQs are very caring and sweet, with a tendency to wear their heart on their sleeves. If they like you, you will be smothered with affection but they can sometimes be clingy and a bit much.

Sweet & Sours are creative free spirits that like to be the focus of attention. They're indecisive and prone to mood swings, but there's never a dull moment in their company. Their fickle tendencies and unpredictability can often land them in sticky situations though.

Hot Sauces are outgoing and boisterous with a fiery temper. They're very stubborn and opinionated, but their opinions are not always welcome. They're fun to be around in small doses, but get on the wrong side of a Hot Sauce and you will certainly know about it.

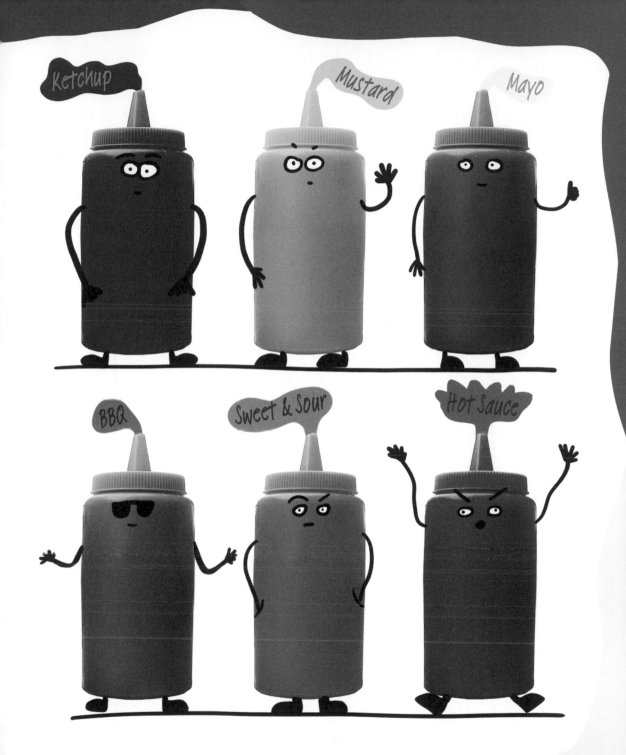

27

NO REGERTS!

These customers have come into your tattoo shop with some unusual requests. Can you give them the artwork that they're after?

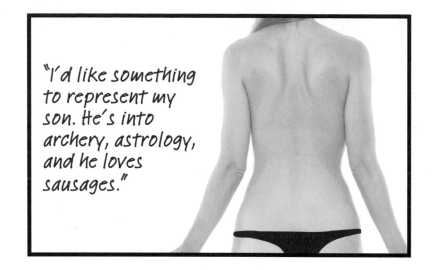

"I'd like something to represent my son. He's into archery, astrology, and he loves sausages."

"I'd like a memorial piece for my pet goldfish Vincent."

"I want a portrait of my beloved pets together. I have a snake, a crab, and a hamster."

"I don't know what I want..."

"I'm after something that portrays my love of making bad decisions."

PEOPLE-WATCHING BINGO

Find yourself a perfect people-watching spot and see how many of these you can tick off.

5 POINTS

10 POINTS

20 POINTS

50 POINTS

PHONE ZOMBIE	COFFEE CLUTCHER	FASHION DISASTER	ELECTRIC SCOOTER
PUBLIC DISPLAY OF AFFECTION	SCREAMING BABY	VAPE PUFFER	UNENJOYABLE EXERCISE
RELUCTANT HAND-HOLDING	INSTA PHOTO SHOOT	BICKERING COUPLE	CELEBRITY LOOKALIKE
BUTT SCRATCHER	AWKWARD FIRST DATE	FINGER SNIFFER	HEADPHONE LIP-SYNCER

YOUR SCORE:

This couple are having renovation regrets. Can you give them a hand decorating?

THE DATING GAME

Use this scientifically proven system to word the perfect bio and improve your online dating success. Just enter the last four digits of your phone number, find your tailored description, and watch the dates come rolling in.

WRITE YOUR DIGITS HERE

I LOOK LIKE...

0. Someone's spilled something on a cardboard cutout.
1. All of ABBA mashed into one.
2. A very human-like robot.
3. A melted waxwork of an attractive raccoon.
4. A half-eaten pastry.
5. A startled badger in a wig.
6. An impressionist sculpture of a foot.
7. A character from the Lord of the Rings.
8. A sun-dried cucumber.
9. An inside-out whoopee cushion.

I ENJOY...

0. Public displays of animosity.
1. Long rides on the bus.
2. Frequent trips to the dentist.
3. Spontaneously starting rap battles with strangers.
4. Working out. (Maths equations. Not in the gym)
5. Pina coladas and getting caught in the rain.
6. Disappointing my parents.
7. Second dates *wink face emoji*.
8. Staring out of a train window pretending I'm in a music video.
9. Finding things I'd forgotten about in jacket pockets.

I WOULD LIKE TO MEET...

0. Anyone. Literally anyone.
1. A dog person. Not a person that likes dogs. A half-dog, half-person hybrid.
2. Someone in need of a project.
3. My partner in crime. No seriously, I'm a very lonely criminal.
4. Someone who can give me legal advice at a competitive rate.
5. A friend. Rachel, Ross, maybe Chandler.
6. Somewhere well lit with CCTV.
7. Someone to eat pickled onions in bed with.
8. Up with my ex-wife. Sharon if you're reading this, please take me back.
9. Gordon Ramsay. He seems nice.

MY JOB INVOLVES...

0. Four things. A good memory, a good memory, and I can't remember the last one.
1. Coming up with serving suggestions on packets of microwavable rice.
2. Guarding the colonel's top-secret herbs and spices recipe.
3. Taste-testing envelope adhesive.
4. Breaking the law several times a day.
5. A lot more effort than I care to part with.
6. Recruiting people for a startup cult.
7. Fighting for my right to party.
8. Matchmaking. In a match factory. I'm not a professional at finding love. Hence why I'm on a dating app.
9. Sending a lot of emails. Mostly to HR.

FUSION CUISINE

Everyone has their own peculiar food pairings that shouldn't work but they do. What are yours?

Fries and Strawberry Milkshake

Cherry Cola and Red Wine

Curry and Mashed Potato

Chocolate Spread on Naan Bread

SPIRIT ANIMALS

Which one of these Spirit Animals do you most identify with?

GINCHILLA

- Chill by name, chill by nature.
- Spontaneous and doesn't care for plans.
- Takes life on the gin.

VODCOW

- Can be a bit mooody.
- Doesn't do much exercise.
- Spends a lot of time eating.
- Very transparent.

RUMMINGBIRD

- An effortlessly class act.
- Sexy and sophisticated.
- Mysterious persona with a light and dark side.
- Elegantly glides through life.

TEQUILAGATOR

- Brings the party at any opportunity.
- Takes life with a pinch of salt.
- Infectious personality.
- Too much of them will leave you with a sore head.

LAMBUCA

- Incredibly sweet and kind.
- Giggles at everything and anything.
- Fun company and easy to get on with.
- They can be naughty but their cuteness means they get away with anything.

WHISKEEL

- A smooth and slippery hustler.
- Blends in and mixes well with others.
- This wise master of disguise can be cunning and devious.
- Loyal to those close, but double-cross them and you'll be left on the rocks.

BRANDEER

- Intellectual and mature.
- Very introverted and prefer their own company.
- They make smart life choices and are often rich.
- Immaculately dressed.

RELATIVELY FAMOUS

You can't choose your family. But if you could, which celebrities would you choose to have as relations?

Bear in mind that whoever you choose must make biological sense in relation to your own age.

GRANDFATHER

GRANDMOTHER

AUNTIE

MOTHER

FATHER

UNCLE

SISTER

BROTHER

COUSIN

SWEET DREAMS
ARE MADE OF... CHEESE?

The first three words that you see will feature in your dreams tonight.

A V S Z M U Z K O L B N H D O O M G S U
B K F C I P B E E S O S N B A P D A V L
G C D B I T C O I N K Z W O R K I U O L
V B I P N U D E S O M U L L E T S K H S
Y T C B O N J O V I G T D C H E E S E P
N C G V U N F B S C O O T E R S D G E Q
E X T S Y K L Q M H R F K J S N W X P T
O T A F R W A P U A P A N D A S G R Z S
U B E Y O N C E R N U Y S B A L L S L H
M U D W R E S T L I N G B N M N A N J L
B X P A S T A F J K G U G F N M P D Y R
S W Y B C A R O L B A S K I N M G B E D
S R F B N H F V C X D I Y H B E A R D S
Y O G A A J F I M E M E S L W B O P I T
N Y R A R H G H O U S E P L A N T S O I
G F R E E D O M H D U S J W P I Z Z A U
M O D G L X R D R A C U L A O Y M G W T
Y E M B G T O A S T L B W N E M Z I R P
F R A U F O S K E O M N H U V J L Z A R
O C A V H M O N E Y L P O L I T I C S J

WHAT A CROP OUT

Things aren't always how they seem on the internet. These cropped images posted online don't show the full picture. Draw in the rest of the scene to show what's really going on.

FANTASY FEST

Curate your ideal festival line-up without limitations.

Want to see that metal Bee-Gees tribute band higher up the bill? Go ahead.

A 3-hour spoken word poetry set to headline the main stage? Why not?

Justin Bieber playing an intimate show in your tent? Ok, steady on.

NAME:
TIME:
PLACE:

MAIN STAGE

STAGE 2

STAGE 3

47

BORED GAME

Each player chooses a random word at least five letters long. They then have to make their way from their house to the treasure using their chosen word's letters in order. Each letter of the alphabet correlates to a number between one and five, as shown at the bottom of this page. If you've reached the end of your word before you get to the treasure, just start from the first letter again. If you don't have any friends, challenge yourself to find a word that gets to the treasure in as few letters as possible.

Here's what to do if you land on a picture square...

█████ You've seen someone up ahead you'd rather not bump into. Retreat three spaces before they turn around and notice you.

█████ Find an abandoned E-scooter and progress three spaces.

█████ Stop to pet a very good boy and miss a go.

█████ You encounter a territorial cat. Move back two spaces to avoid.

█████ A volatile pensioner starts yelling abuse at you. Run past quickly and progress three spaces.

█████ Ducks crossing the road. Miss a go while you wait for them to reach the other side safely.

█████ Magic portal. If your next letter is a five, move to any of the other magic portals on the board.

█████ Coffee pitstop. You're now full of beans. On your next turn, double your letter's value.

█████ Get disorientated in a vape cloud. Skip your next letter.

A – 3	E – 1	I – 2	M – 4	Q – 5	U – 3	Y – 1
B – 4	F – 2	J – 2	N – 1	R – 4	V – 4	Z – 5
C – 2	G – 3	K – 4	O – 4	S – 3	W – 3	
D – 5	H – 4	L – 3	P – 2	T – 2	X – 5	

TREASURE

PLAYER 1'S HOUSE

PLAYER 2'S HOUSE

49

UNMEMORABLE INFORMATION

You're one step away from purchasing that dream blender that you just saw on a shopping channel, but as it's the sixth impulse purchase of the afternoon you're going to need to answer some security questions before proceeding to checkout. Write your answers and get that blender before it's gone!

Least desired condiment:

Your arch nemesis:

That film you love to hate:

Your ideal date location:

Your go-to toast topping:

A nostalgic childhood cereal:

That song you shouldn't like
but you do:

Longest-standing food item in
the back of your cupboard:

PROCEED TO CHECKOUT

LIFE COACHING LLAMA

Assuming the role of the Life Coaching Llama, can you respond to these letters with some words of advice?

Dear LCL,

I've become quite concerned for a duck in my local park as it seems to be being bullied by the other ducks. I'm planning a rescue mission to save said duck. How should I go about it?

Brenda

Dear LCL,

I'm etrified of a certain letter in the alhabet. I just can't bring myself to ronounce or write it and it's becoming quite a roblem. lease hel me.

Thanks,
eter

I've developed feelings for the Amazon delivery man, so I keep ordering things online just so that I can see him again. All the online shopping is getting me into financial trouble but it's worth it for that brief encounter. How do I tell him how I feel?

Anonymous

BUCKET LIST

Write a list of all the useful things you can do with a bucket.

55

PUN PROMPTS

Put your punning skills to the test and fill these tables with your best plays on words.

	MOVIE TITLE	MUSIC ARTIST	COMEDIAN NAME	SONG TITLE
FAST FOOD ITEM			BILL BURR-ITO	
TYPE OF CAKE				
KITCHEN UTENSIL	SPATU-LA LA LAND			
FRUIT AND VEG				

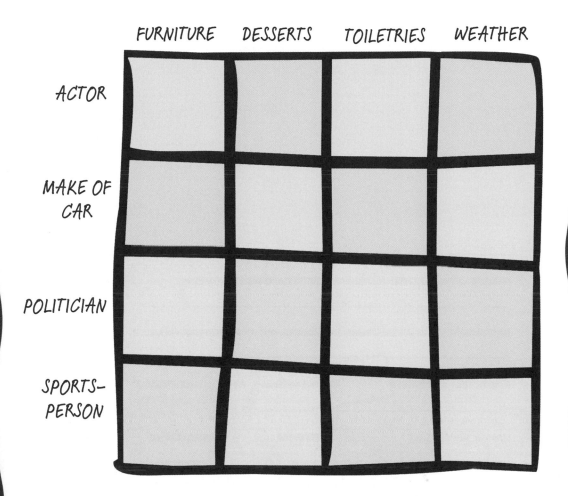

	FURNITURE	DESSERTS	TOILETRIES	WEATHER
ACTOR				
MAKE OF CAR				
POLITICIAN				
SPORTS- PERSON				

WELCOME TO THE JUMBLE!

Smash two animals together and come up with your own animal hybrid creations.

59

BRUNCH BREAKDOWN

Help this confused customer decide on his brunch order using your initials and your birth month.

First initial

Last initial

Birth month

A = Pumpkin Spiced
B = Moon Dried
C = Slightly Smashed
D = Quadruple Cooked
E = Double Rubbed
F = Sweetly Serenaded
G = Cosmopolitan
H = Part Fermented
I = De-robed
J = Reclaimed
K = Spoon Fed
L = Feather Dusted
M = Gently Tickled

N = Hand Crimped
O = Vine Ripened
P = Chauffeur Driven
Q = Tenderly Massaged
R = Lightly Soiled
S = Cold Pressed
T = Ego Stroked
U = Reconstructed
V = Velvetized
W = Air Glazed
X = Loose Leaf
Y = Overindulged
Z = Upcycled

A = Avocado Ball
B = Sesame Milk
C = Carrot Origami
D = Turmeric Residue
E = Goji Blossom
F = Quail Egg
G = Lemon Teardrop
H = Sea Foam
I = Couscous
J = Jack Fruit Essence
K = Sushi Lining
L = Sourdough Crouton
M = Jazz Apple

N = Pea Petal
O = Matcha Dust
P = Beetroot Ink
Q = Artichoke Pulp
R = Kiwi Hair
S = Leftover Hummus
T = Peony Extract
U = Liquorice Wrapper
V = Salmon Rind
W = Geranium Bulb
X = Quinoa Grain
Y = Dandelion Stem
Z = Bamboo Branch

Jan = On toast
Feb = Frapuccino
Mar = Panini
Apr = Truffles

May = Sorbet
Jun = Chutney
Jul = Medley
Aug = Ciabatta

Sep = Linguine
Oct = Bagel
Nov = Latte
Dec = Smoothie

F FOR PHONETIC

The current phonetic alphabet is outdated and hard to remember. Think up your own version then try it out on an unsuspecting phone operator.

A =   N =

B =   O =

C =   P =

D =   Q =

E =   R =

F =   S =

G =   T =

H =   U =

I =   V =

J =   W =

K =   X =

L =   Y =

M =   Z =

HOUSE PURRRTY

Which of these party-goers do you most relate to?

SOCIAL MEDIA BINGO

Have a scroll through your social media feed and see how many of these you encounter.

5 POINTS

10 POINTS

20 POINTS

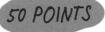

50 POINTS

MEME	ANIMAL	SCENIC VIEW	#AD
FOOD PORN	PARTIAL NUDITY	HOLIDAY BRAGGING	SPORTING ACTIVITY
INSPIRING QUOTE	BEARDED MAN SELFIE	ATTENTION SEEKING	OVER 12 HASHTAGS ON ONE POST
SOMETHING YOU WISH YOU COULD UNSEE	EVIDENCE THAT MIGHT LATER BE RELIED ON IN COURT	AN UTTERLY USELESS "LIFE HACK"	ESCALATING BEEF IN THE COMMENT SECTION

YOUR SCORE:

THEMED MIXTAPES

Create some themed playlists using the categories written on each cassette tape.

ANIMALS

1. EYE OF THE TIGER

1. SWEET CHILD O' MINE

FAMILY

1. YELLOW SUBMARINE

MODES OF TRANSPORT

THE DEVIL WEARS PASTA

World-renowned fashion designer Penne Tagliatelle has created a spagtacular outfit for this year's fashion awards ceremony.

As somewhat of a fashionista yourself, you've been asked to create next year's iconic look.

Design an unusual outfit that will turn heads on the red carpet, then give your new clothing label a fitting name.

IT'S TAGLIATELLE, DARLING!

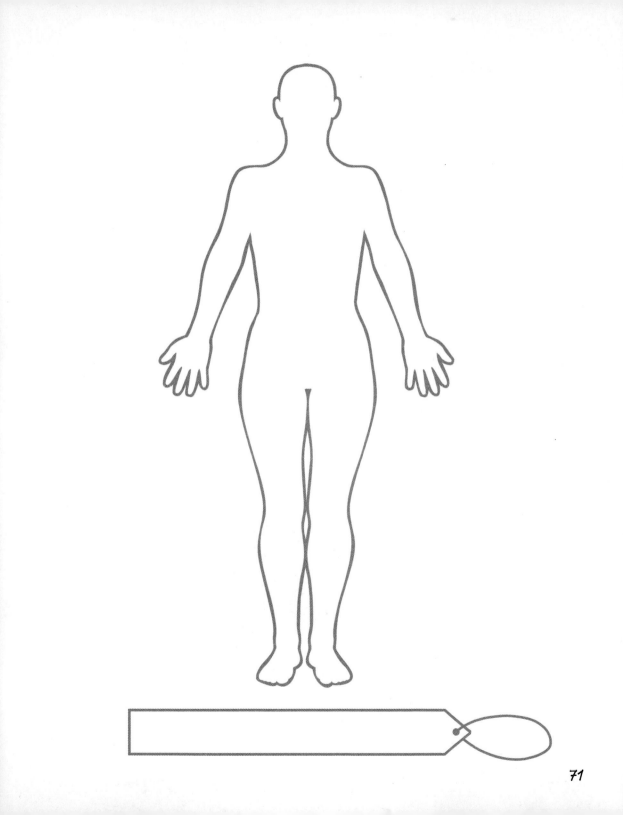

71

...AAAND ACTION!

Create a poster for the film of your life.

Some things to think about...

- What would the title of the film be?
- What would the tagline be?
- Who would play you in the lead role?
- Who would also feature in the film?
- What genre would the film be?
- What images would best represent the film?

73

GET IN THE CANNON

Choose some things that you think should be put in to a big cannon and fired off the face of the earth.

People who disagree with me on Twitter

Bluetooth when it doesn't connect

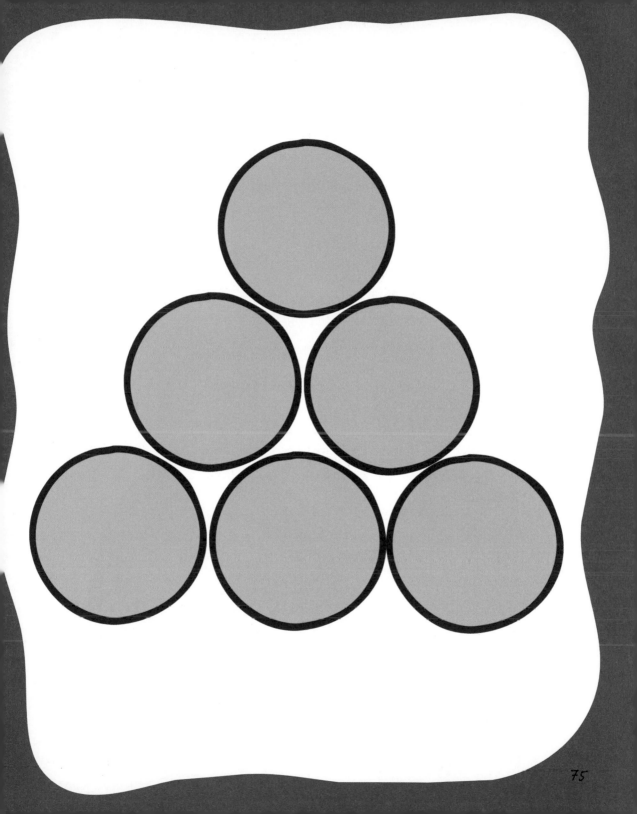

AND THE WINNER IS...

Create your own awards ceremony and nominate your friends and family. Think of some unusual categories, then decide the most fitting winner for each.

RANDOM EMAIL GENERATOR

For when your Monday mind goes blank.

Use the last five digits of your phone number to word the perfect reply.

Write your numbers in here

```
0 = Hello there          5 = Listen up
1 = Greetings            6 = Hiya
2 = Sup                  7 = Look here, pal
3 = Yo                   8 = Good day
4 = Howdy                9 = Namaste
```

```
0 = I admire             5 = I'd normally appreciate
1 = I agree with         6 = I'm worried about
2 = I can relate to      7 = I'm a bit concerned with
3 = I understand         8 = I'm confused with
4 = I respect            9 = I would love to know
                             more about
```

```
0 = That thing you just said
1 = Your new haircut
2 = Your passion for life
3 = Your outfit choice
4 = Your thesis on flat-earth theory
5 = Your thoughts on veganism
6 = Your confidence on camera
7 = How much you care about this matter
8 = That voice note you left me
9 = Your last social media post
```

However...

```
0 = I'm busy having a meltdown
1 = My pet needs attention
2 = I'm currently naked from the waist down
3 = I'm busy playing Candy Crush
4 = I'm busy planning my own surprise party
5 = This is probably a matter for HR
6 = I'm on the cusp of a scientific breakthrough
7 = My shopping list won't write itself
8 = I've just pulled a muscle recreating
    something I saw on TikTok
9 = I don't think that attachment was meant for me
```

```
0 = Please don't reply       5 = Mic drop
1 = Don't contact me again   6 = Peace out
2 = Unkind regards           7 = Hugs and kisses
3 = Seasons Greetings        8 = Good to chat
4 = Hope that helps          9 = Remove me from
                                 your contacts
```

<Your Name>

MAKE YOUR DEBUT

Design the artwork for your album cover. Think up a stage name that sums you up, an apt title for your body of work, as well as a list of tracks featuring any dream collaborations.

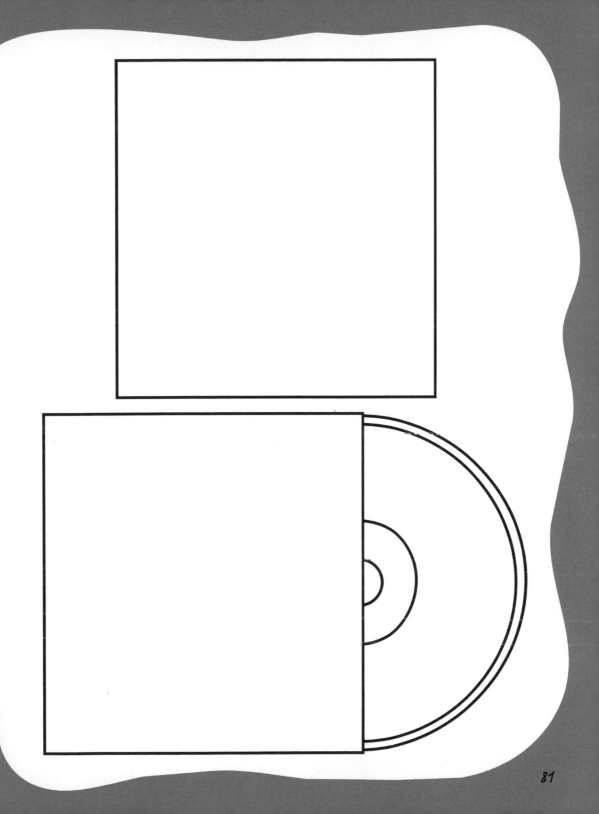

UNINSPIRING QUOTES

Come up with some dismally demotivational quotes to adorn your walls. For those days when you wake up feeling a bit too chipper and need a harsh dose of reality.

LIFE'S TOO LONG

IT'S ALL DOWNHILL FROM HERE

EAT. POOP. REPEAT.

WHY BOTHER?

TODAY WILL BE AS UNEVENTFUL AS YESTERDAY

YOUR PET ONLY LIKES YOU BECAUSE YOU FEED IT

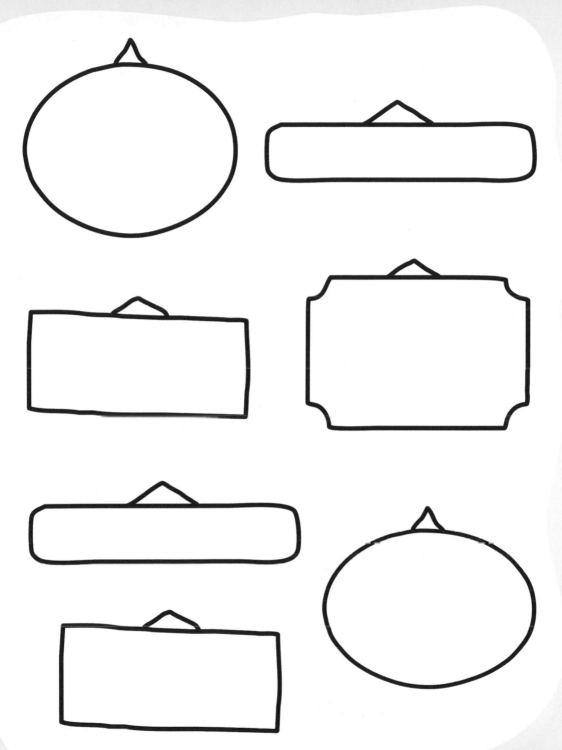

RUSHIN' ROULETTE

Next time you're in a hurry to leave the house but can't decide on an outfit to wear, use this wheel and put your sartorial decision in the hands of fate.

Either spin your pen in the middle of the wheel, or simply prop this book against your wardrobe and chuck pens at it until you have enough clothing items to make up a catwalk worthy outfit.

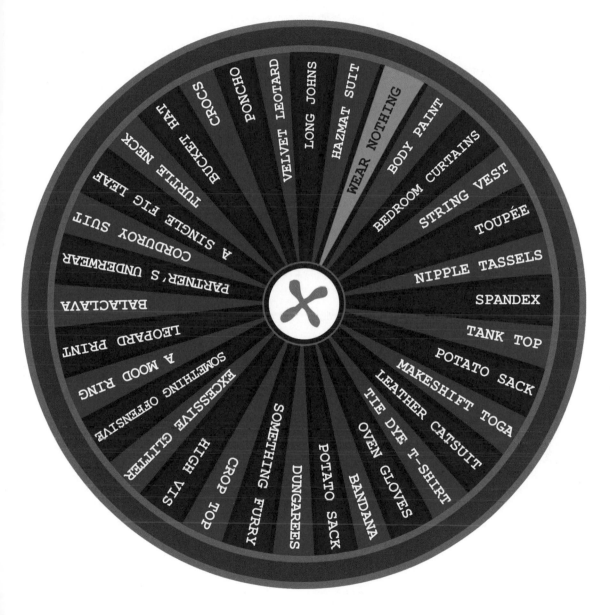

85

INTERNAL THOUGHTS

Write in the speech bubbles what the people in these scenes are actually thinking.

IMAGINATION

VS.

REALITY

WHERE YOU ARE

WHERE YOU'D RATHER BE

VS.

WHAT YOU'RE DOING

WHAT YOU'D RATHER BE DOING

VS.

WHAT YOU'RE WEARING

WHAT YOU'D RATHER BE WEARING

VS.

NON-SCENTS

If you were tasked with creating your own line of scented candles, what would they be called and what sort of smells would you bottle up to put in them?

91

ON A SCALE OF...

Put a mark on these scales where you'd place yourself.

WARM SPOON THROUGH AN ICE CREAM

MOOSE ON ROLLERSKATES

HOW SMOOTH ARE YOU?

SOYA MILK ON BRAN FLAKES

FLAMING SAMBUCA ON FROOT LOOPS

HOW MUCH OF A MORNING PERSON ARE YOU?

TOE NAILS

SCALP

WHAT'S YOUR BEST BODILY ASSET?

IRONING BOARD — HOW RAD ARE YOU? — SURF BOARD

BLANK CANVAS — HOW ARTISTIC ARE YOU? — PABLO VAN POLLOCK

"IS THIS THE REAL LIFE?" — WHICH PART OF BOHEMIAN RHAPSODY ARE YOU? — "SCARAMOUCH! SCARAMOUCH! CAN YOU DO THE FANDANGO?"

SNOW WHITE — HOW INNOCENT ARE YOU? — WALTER WHITE

NEW NAME, WHO DIS?

You never know when you might need to change your identity at a moment's notice, so use these methods to conjure up some alias options.

First name of the last
singer you listened to
+
The last thing you ate

A childhood pet's name
+
The last name of a teacher
you disliked at school

First name of the last
TV chef you watched
+
The most used spice
in your cupboard

Your flower of choice
+
The element in the periodic table
that corresponds to your age

First name that comes into your
head beginning with your first initial
+
First word that comes into your
head beginning with your first initial

A WORLD OF YOUR OWN

You're running for leader of the world. Write down a winning manifesto that will be sure to land you the job.

MY MANIFESTO

7 BREADLY SINS

Which of the seven sins is being depicted in each of the following bread-based scenarios?

GLUTTONY

LUST

SLOTH

ENVY

PRIDE

GREED

WRATH

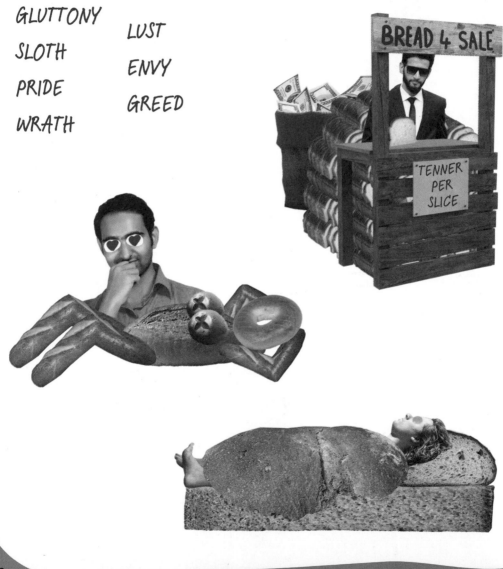

DOGGO DIARY

Your canine associate Lord Woofington of Barkshire has many important activities and engagements to keep track of on a daily basis. As his personal assistant, it's down to you to make a note of them. Write a to-do list that reflects the day in the life of this Very Important Pooch.

6 DEGREES OF SEPARATION

This game starts with two random and unrelated words. You must get from one to the other using exactly six associated words.

GRAPEFRUIT

SEEDS
FLOWERS
LEAVES
FALLING
ASLEEP
BED

PILLOW

NOSE

EARS
HEARD
HERD
ELEPHANTS
TRUNK
STORAGE

PADLOCK

ROOF

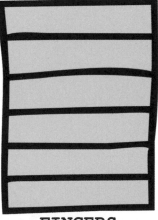

FINGERS

TABLE

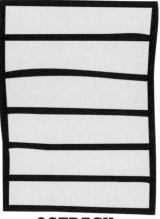

OSTRICH

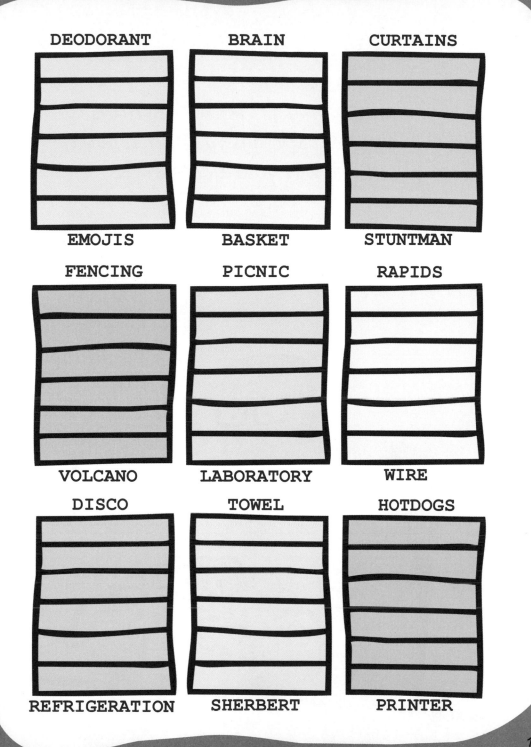

DEODORANT   BRAIN   CURTAINS

EMOJIS   BASKET   STUNTMAN

FENCING   PICNIC   RAPIDS

VOLCANO   LABORATORY   WIRE

DISCO   TOWEL   HOTDOGS

REFRIGERATION   SHERBERT   PRINTER

FILL IN ___ BLANKS

Write in the missing words from these sentences with the first thing that springs to mind. It could reveal a lot about the way your brain works.

It's hard to _____ when you're _____.

Sometimes after _____ I like to _____ in front of _____.

You shouldn't _____ before _____.

And you definitely shouldn't _____ during _____.

_____ is much more fun when _____.

I haven't _____ since _____.

I enjoy _____ but only when _____.

Sometimes when I'm _____ I just can't resist _____.

Life is just a series of _____ .

FOOD FOR THOUGHT

If you could cast that restrictive diet to one side and forget your own culinary limitations, what would your dream three-course meal consist of?

The food can come from anywhere and be prepared by anyone. Each course is also accompanied by a different drink of your choice.

STARTER

MAIN

DESSERT

ONE HOUR OF POWER

If you could have one hour's worth of super powers a week, what would they be and how would you divide them up?

You can't save time up, and the watch resets every Sunday at midnight.

Turn anything into hash browns

Fingers become Nerf guns

Predict five mins into the future

Turn into a wafer and slip through cracks

Put people on mute IRL

Really good at yo-yo

Skin becomes tasty pastry

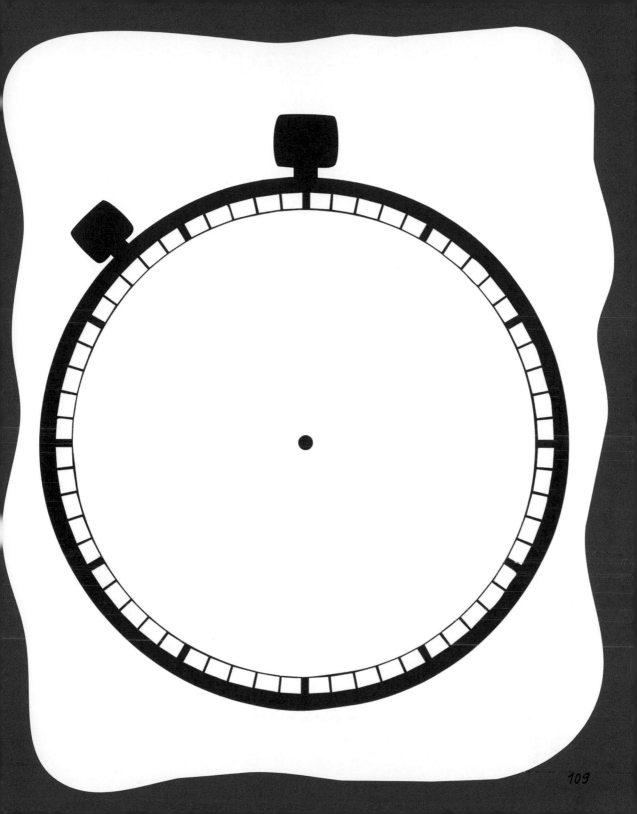

THE ART OF PASSIVE-AGGRESSIVE NOTE LEAVING

Whether it's to ward off a roommate from that leftover slice of pizza, or a polite reminder not to park in front of your prize pansies, the passive-aggressive note has many uses. Word the perfect notes to help restore some order in this chaotic communal kitchen.

YOUR PODCAST SCRIPT

Use the following information to work out the intro for your podcast.

(A) <A grandparent's forename + something in your house starting with the same letter>

(B) "<The last three words of the last text you sent>"

(C) <An inanimate object from the tenth photo in your camera reel + the letters "-ify">

(D) <Current phone battery percentage>

(E) <The first thing you'd say if you won the lottery, all in caps with no spaces>

(F) <The coolest kid at your first school + a planet>

(G) <The last thing you dreamt about>

(H) <Your mother's birth decade>

(I) <One of the first five people in your social media feed>

(J) <The subject matter of their latest post>

(K) <Your current mood>

(L) <Verb starting with the same letter as mood + "ing">

Hi, I'm _____(A)_____

and welcome to "_____(B)_____"

This episode is brought to you by _____(C)_____.

For _(D)_% off your first order, use the discount
code _____(E)_____

Today we're joined by _____(F)_____,
an expert on _____(G)_____ in the _(H)_.

In this episode, we'll be discussing _____(I)_____,
star of the new Netflix series "The _____(J)_____
Scandal".

Thanks for listening. Remember to stay _____(K)_____
and keep _____(L)_____.

WEAPON OF MILD DISTRACTION

Build your best DIY catapult then put it to the test.

This catapult was built using wooden cutlery, hair-ties, and a piece of scrap card, but you can use whatever similar items you can find about the house.

Use these instructions to get you started in the right direction, but you should approach your construction with a certain amount of "make it up as you go along." Obey the laws of physics and see what you can come up with.

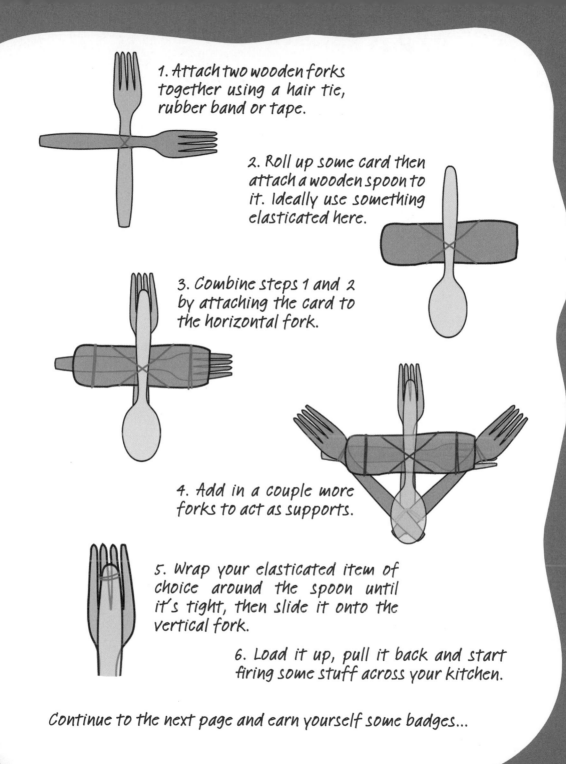

1. Attach two wooden forks together using a hair tie, rubber band or tape.

2. Roll up some card then attach a wooden spoon to it. Ideally use something elasticated here.

3. Combine steps 1 and 2 by attaching the card to the horizontal fork.

4. Add in a couple more forks to act as supports.

5. Wrap your elasticated item of choice around the spoon until it's tight, then slide it onto the vertical fork.

6. Load it up, pull it back and start firing some stuff across your kitchen.

Continue to the next page and earn yourself some badges...

Once you've constructed your mini feat of engineering from the previous page, see how many of these badges you can achieve.

DIY CONSTRUCTION LEVEL 1
Well done on completing your catapult build. Have a badge.

PRECISION & ACCURACY
Catapult three teabags into a mug and you'll earn this badge, and a cup of tea.

TALL ORDER
Fire a pea or similar item over the tallest thing you can.

GO LONG

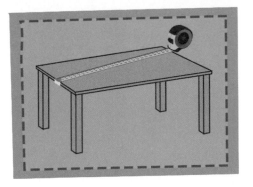

Propel your chosen object and see how far you can get it. Placing your catapult at an angle will help you to cover more distance.

AIR TIME

Get up high, load up something light and see how long it takes for it to reach the ground.

PROCRASTINATION CERTIFICATION

Well that killed some time. Have a badge for some top notch procrastination and get back to whatever it is you've been putting off for the last hour.

CATS RULE

If cats had the dexterity to hold a pencil in their paws, they'd probably write up a list of house rules for their human cohabitants to abide by.

Write down what you think would be on that list.

CORPORATE SQUAWK

Business types love to make up their own spiel and hurl it around the boardroom. It's often comprised of nonsensical buzzwords and corporate jargon that baffles anyone on the receiving end. Write down your best biz chat that would be sure to land you that big promotion. This is a safe space to "unpack", "circle back", and "align" to your heart's content.

PARCEL PUZZLE

Help this delivery driver get your parcel to its safe place.

Your Parcel

With that weird guy next door

At your local depot 42km away

Not so safe place

Left with your pet

Safe Place

ARTIST UNKNOWN

Create a work of art using the title as inspiration.

"Inappropriate Vegetables"
by _____ Age __

FAKE NEWS!

It's a slow news day today, but you're a journalist at "The Daily Rhymes" newspaper and you need to come up with something to fill the pages.

At "The Daily Rhymes" you're allowed to make up headlines, so long as the perpetrator rhymes with the alleged news about them. See what you can come up with while you wait for something interesting to happen.

Well, that's it. Thanks for stopping by and relieving some boredom. Time to get back to doing whatever it is you were doing before you opened this book.

Share your answers and creations online using #OpenThisBook.

ACKNOWLEDGMENTS

All artwork has been made using images from Pixabay, an amazing source of stock media. Thanks to Annie Brumsen, Sarah Jennings, Vanessa Daubney and the team at Arcturus for bringing this book to life.